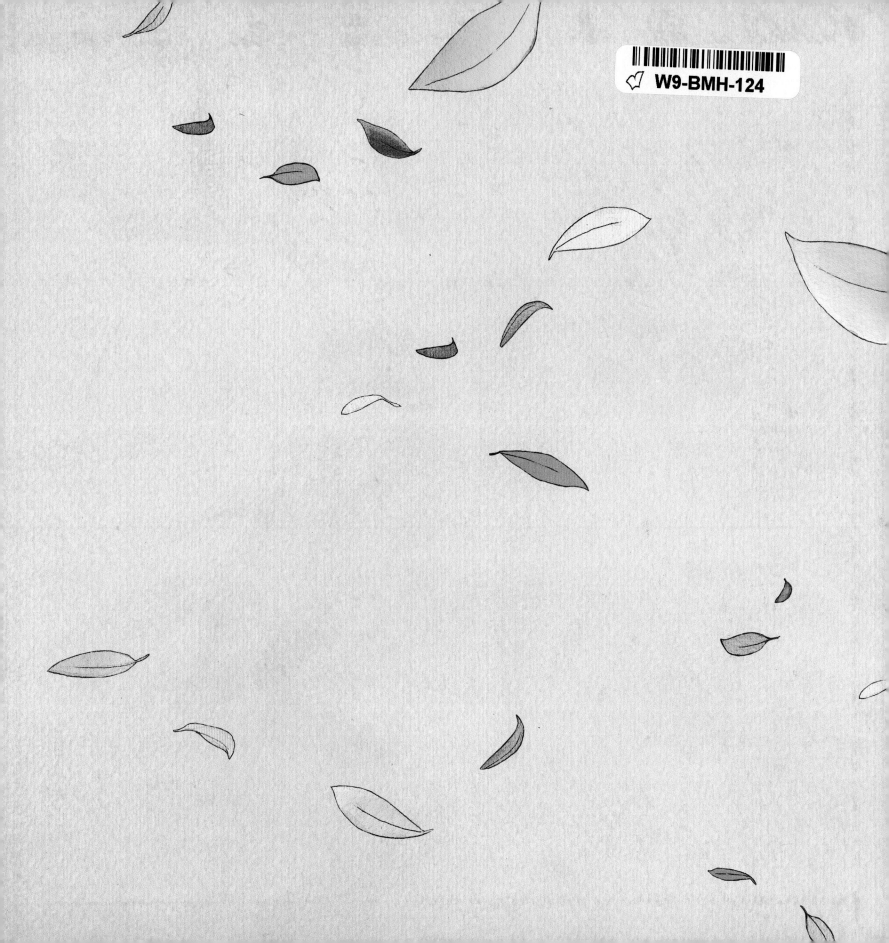

The Windy Day

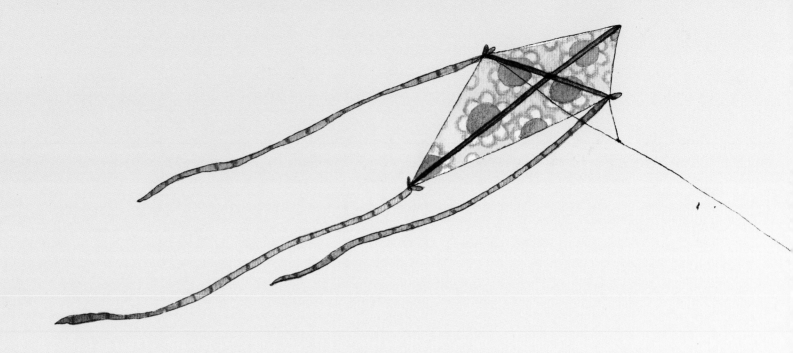

Edited by Gillian Doherty.
With thanks to Dr. Roger Brugge,
from the Department of Meteorology, Reading University,
for information about the wind.

First published in 2007 by Usborne Publishing Ltd, 83-85 Saffron Hill, London EC1N 8RT, England.
www.usborne.com Copyright © 2007 Usborne Publishing Ltd. The name Usborne and the
devices ⊕ ⊕ are Trade Marks of Usborne Publishing Ltd. All rights reserved. No part of this
publication may be reproduced, stored in a retrieval system, or transmitted in any form or
by any means, electronic, mechanical, photocopying, recording or otherwise,
without the prior permission of the publisher.
First published in America in 2007. UE. Printed in Dubai.

The Windy Day

Anna Milbourne

Illustrated by Elena Temporin

Designed by Laura Parker

Have you ever wondered what sways the trees...

and makes leaves dance across the grass?

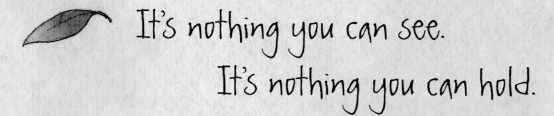

It's nothing you can see.
It's nothing you can hold.

But if you go outside on a windy day, you can feel it.

It's the air moving around.
It ruffles your hair...

and snatches your hat,
almost as if it wants to play.

If you roll out the string
of a big, bright kite...

then throw the kite into the air
and run as fast as you can...

...the wind might catch it
and make it fly.

It dips and dives and swoops around...

held up by the invisible wind.

All at once,
a blustery gust
tosses the kite into a tree.

The wind is rough-and-tumbly along the cliff.
It rushes in from the sea and stumbles over the bumpy land.

But out on the open sea...

the wind blows steadily for miles and miles.

It fills a boat's sails,

making them billow,

and pushes the boat

across the waves.

High in the sky, seagulls cry...

and their voices are carried
away by the wind.

They tilt their wings to catch the breeze,
and ride it back to shore.

It's too blowy for little birds to fly around.

So they huddle up on a branch
and wait for the wind to go away.

At the foot of the tree
there's a sheltered spot...

where animals hide from the chilly wind,
tucked into holes and piles of fallen leaves.

As the wind rustles a sycamore tree,
its twirly seeds are shaken free.

They spin down...

and down...

and down.

The seeds lie scattered on the ground.
Soon they'll start to grow into new sycamore trees.

Further along the clifftops
stands a row of tall, white windmills.

Wind blowing in from the sea
slowly pushes their sails around.

The turning windmills make electricity
which is sent through wires to a nearby town.

It lights up the lights there
and makes all kinds of things work.

You might wonder if the restless wind
ever gets tired of blowing.

But even when the wind
dies down where you are...

...it's always blowing
somewhere.